50 Fresh Salads for Every Season

By: Kelly Johnson

Table of Contents

- Classic Caesar Salad
- Greek Salad
- Caprese Salad
- Autumn Harvest Salad
- Quinoa and Roasted Vegetable Salad
- Watermelon and Feta Salad
- Cobb Salad
- Arugula and Pear Salad
- Southwest Chicken Salad
- Roasted Beet and Goat Cheese Salad
- Kale and Apple Salad
- Chickpea and Cucumber Salad
- Avocado and Mango Salad
- Spinach and Strawberry Salad
- Roasted Sweet Potato Salad
- Asian Sesame Salad
- Tuna Nicoise Salad
- Mediterranean Orzo Salad
- Thai Peanut Salad
- Grilled Peach and Burrata Salad
- Broccoli and Bacon Salad
- Grilled Corn and Tomato Salad
- Panzanella (Italian Bread Salad)
- Apple and Walnut Salad
- Farro and Roasted Carrot Salad
- Beetroot and Walnut Salad
- Brussels Sprout and Pomegranate Salad
- Cabbage and Radish Slaw
- Shrimp and Avocado Salad
- Lemon and Herb Potato Salad
- Grilled Zucchini and Halloumi Salad
- Cucumber, Dill, and Yogurt Salad
- Carrot and Chickpea Salad
- Poppy Seed and Apple Salad
- Roasted Brussels Sprout Salad

- Spinach and Bacon Salad
- Warm Lentil Salad with Goat Cheese
- Grilled Chicken and Mango Salad
- Roasted Cauliflower and Tahini Salad
- Fennel and Orange Salad
- Spinach and Quinoa Salad
- Roasted Pumpkin and Kale Salad
- Strawberry and Almond Salad
- Roasted Vegetable and Couscous Salad
- Shrimp and Grapefruit Salad
- Lentil and Avocado Salad
- Cucumber and Tomato Salad
- Apple, Beet, and Walnut Salad
- Pear and Blue Cheese Salad
- Roasted Tomato and Pesto Salad

Classic Caesar Salad

Ingredients:

- 4 cups Romaine lettuce, chopped
- 1 cup croutons
- 1/2 cup grated Parmesan cheese
- 1/4 cup Caesar dressing (store-bought or homemade)
- 1 teaspoon anchovy paste (optional)

Instructions:

1. **Prepare the Lettuce:**
    - Wash and chop the Romaine lettuce. Dry thoroughly.
2. **Assemble the Salad:**
    - In a large bowl, combine the lettuce, croutons, and Parmesan cheese.
3. **Dress the Salad:**
    - Toss with Caesar dressing and anchovy paste (if using).
4. **Serve:**
    - Serve immediately as a starter or side dish.

Greek Salad

Ingredients:

- 2 cups cucumber, diced
- 2 cups cherry tomatoes, halved
- 1 red onion, thinly sliced
- 1/2 cup Kalamata olives
- 1/2 cup feta cheese, crumbled or in blocks
- 1/4 cup olive oil
- 2 tablespoons red wine vinegar
- 1 teaspoon dried oregano
- Salt and pepper, to taste

Instructions:

1. **Prepare the Vegetables:**
    - Slice cucumber, tomatoes, and red onion.
2. **Combine the Ingredients:**
    - In a large bowl, toss the cucumber, tomatoes, onion, olives, and feta cheese.
3. **Make the Dressing:**
    - In a small bowl, whisk together olive oil, red wine vinegar, oregano, salt, and pepper.
4. **Dress and Serve:**
    - Pour the dressing over the salad, toss gently, and serve immediately.

Caprese Salad

Ingredients:

- 4 large tomatoes, sliced
- 8 ounces fresh mozzarella, sliced
- 1/4 cup fresh basil leaves
- 1/4 cup extra virgin olive oil
- 2 tablespoons balsamic glaze
- Salt and pepper, to taste

Instructions:

1. **Assemble the Salad:**
    - Alternate layers of sliced tomatoes, mozzarella, and basil on a serving platter.
2. **Drizzle and Season:**
    - Drizzle with olive oil and balsamic glaze. Season with salt and pepper.
3. **Serve:**
    - Serve immediately as a fresh, light salad.

Autumn Harvest Salad

Ingredients:

- 4 cups mixed greens (arugula, spinach, kale)
- 1 cup roasted butternut squash
- 1/2 cup pomegranate seeds
- 1/2 cup goat cheese, crumbled
- 1/4 cup pecans, toasted
- 1/4 cup balsamic vinaigrette

Instructions:

1. **Prepare the Salad Base:**
    - Wash and dry the mixed greens.
2. **Add the Roasted Vegetables:**
    - Toss the greens with roasted butternut squash and pomegranate seeds.
3. **Top and Dress:**
    - Sprinkle goat cheese and toasted pecans over the salad. Drizzle with balsamic vinaigrette.
4. **Serve:**
    - Toss gently and serve immediately.

Quinoa and Roasted Vegetable Salad

Ingredients:

- 1 cup quinoa, cooked
- 1 cup roasted vegetables (zucchini, bell peppers, red onions)
- 1/4 cup fresh parsley, chopped
- 2 tablespoons olive oil
- 1 tablespoon lemon juice
- Salt and pepper, to taste

Instructions:

1. **Cook the Quinoa:**
    - Cook quinoa according to package instructions and let cool.
2. **Roast the Vegetables:**
    - Roast diced vegetables in olive oil at 400°F (200°C) for 20-25 minutes until tender.
3. **Combine:**
    - Toss the quinoa with the roasted vegetables and fresh parsley.
4. **Dress and Serve:**
    - Drizzle with olive oil and lemon juice, season with salt and pepper, and serve.

Watermelon and Feta Salad

Ingredients:

- 4 cups watermelon, cubed
- 1/2 cup feta cheese, crumbled
- 1/4 cup fresh mint leaves, chopped
- 1 tablespoon olive oil
- 1 tablespoon lime juice
- Salt and pepper, to taste

Instructions:

1. **Prepare the Ingredients:**
   - Cube the watermelon and crumble the feta.
2. **Assemble the Salad:**
   - In a bowl, combine watermelon, feta, and mint.
3. **Dress and Serve:**
   - Drizzle with olive oil and lime juice, season with salt and pepper, and toss gently. Serve chilled.

Cobb Salad

Ingredients:

- 4 cups mixed greens (romaine, iceberg, arugula)
- 2 cooked chicken breasts, chopped
- 2 hard-boiled eggs, chopped
- 1/2 avocado, sliced
- 1/2 cup cherry tomatoes, halved
- 1/2 cup blue cheese, crumbled
- 1/4 cup bacon, crumbled
- 1/4 cup red wine vinaigrette

Instructions:

1. **Prepare the Salad Base:**
    - Arrange the mixed greens on a large platter.
2. **Add the Toppings:**
    - Arrange rows of chicken, eggs, avocado, tomatoes, blue cheese, and bacon over the greens.
3. **Dress and Serve:**
    - Drizzle with vinaigrette and serve immediately.

Arugula and Pear Salad

Ingredients:

- 4 cups arugula
- 2 pears, sliced
- 1/4 cup walnuts, toasted
- 1/4 cup goat cheese, crumbled
- 2 tablespoons olive oil
- 1 tablespoon balsamic vinegar
- Salt and pepper, to taste

Instructions:

1. **Prepare the Ingredients:**
    - Wash and dry the arugula, slice the pears, and toast the walnuts.
2. **Assemble the Salad:**
    - Toss arugula with pear slices, toasted walnuts, and goat cheese.
3. **Dress and Serve:**
    - Drizzle with olive oil and balsamic vinegar, season with salt and pepper, and serve immediately.

Southwest Chicken Salad

Ingredients:

- 4 cups romaine lettuce, chopped
- 2 cooked chicken breasts, sliced
- 1 cup corn kernels (fresh or frozen)
- 1/2 cup black beans, rinsed and drained
- 1/2 cup diced tomatoes
- 1/4 cup red onion, thinly sliced
- 1/4 cup cilantro, chopped
- 1/4 cup shredded cheddar cheese
- 1/4 cup lime vinaigrette or southwest dressing

Instructions:

1. **Prepare the Salad Base:**
   - Wash and chop the romaine lettuce.
2. **Add the Toppings:**
   - Layer chicken, corn, black beans, tomatoes, red onion, and cilantro on top of the lettuce.
3. **Top and Dress:**
   - Sprinkle with shredded cheddar cheese and drizzle with lime vinaigrette or southwest dressing.
4. **Serve:**
   - Toss gently and serve immediately.

Roasted Beet and Goat Cheese Salad

Ingredients:

- 4 medium beets, peeled and roasted
- 4 cups mixed greens (arugula, spinach, etc.)
- 1/2 cup goat cheese, crumbled
- 1/4 cup walnuts, toasted
- 1/4 cup balsamic vinegar
- 2 tablespoons olive oil
- Salt and pepper, to taste

Instructions:

1. **Roast the Beets:**
    - Preheat the oven to 400°F (200°C). Wrap beets in foil and roast for 45-60 minutes until tender. Peel and slice them.
2. **Prepare the Salad:**
    - In a large bowl, toss the mixed greens, roasted beets, goat cheese, and walnuts.
3. **Dress and Serve:**
    - Drizzle with olive oil and balsamic vinegar. Season with salt and pepper, then toss gently and serve immediately.

Kale and Apple Salad

Ingredients:

- 4 cups kale, chopped and massaged
- 1 red apple, thinly sliced
- 1/4 cup dried cranberries
- 1/4 cup walnuts, chopped
- 1/4 cup feta cheese, crumbled
- 2 tablespoons olive oil
- 1 tablespoon apple cider vinegar
- 1 teaspoon honey
- Salt and pepper, to taste

Instructions:

1. **Massage the Kale:**
   - Wash and chop the kale. Massage with olive oil for about 2 minutes to soften.
2. **Assemble the Salad:**
   - Toss kale with sliced apple, cranberries, walnuts, and feta.
3. **Make the Dressing:**
   - In a small bowl, whisk together apple cider vinegar, honey, salt, and pepper.
4. **Dress and Serve:**
   - Drizzle the dressing over the salad, toss, and serve immediately.

Chickpea and Cucumber Salad

Ingredients:

- 2 cups cooked chickpeas (or 1 can, drained and rinsed)
- 1 cucumber, diced
- 1/2 red onion, thinly sliced
- 1/4 cup fresh parsley, chopped
- 2 tablespoons olive oil
- 1 tablespoon lemon juice
- Salt and pepper, to taste

Instructions:

1. **Combine the Ingredients:**
    - In a large bowl, combine chickpeas, cucumber, red onion, and parsley.
2. **Dress the Salad:**
    - Drizzle with olive oil and lemon juice. Season with salt and pepper.
3. **Serve:**
    - Toss gently and serve immediately.

Avocado and Mango Salad

Ingredients:

- 2 ripe avocados, diced
- 1 mango, peeled and diced
- 1/2 red onion, thinly sliced
- 1/4 cup cilantro, chopped
- 1 lime, juiced
- Salt and pepper, to taste

Instructions:

1. **Prepare the Ingredients:**
   - Dice the avocados and mango, slice the red onion, and chop the cilantro.
2. **Assemble the Salad:**
   - Combine the avocado, mango, onion, and cilantro in a bowl.
3. **Dress and Serve:**
   - Drizzle with lime juice and season with salt and pepper. Toss gently and serve immediately.

Spinach and Strawberry Salad

Ingredients:

- 4 cups fresh spinach
- 1 cup strawberries, sliced
- 1/4 cup goat cheese, crumbled
- 1/4 cup almonds, sliced or chopped
- 2 tablespoons balsamic vinegar
- 1 tablespoon olive oil
- Salt and pepper, to taste

Instructions:

1. **Prepare the Salad Base:**
     - Wash and dry the spinach. Slice the strawberries.
2. **Assemble the Salad:**
     - In a bowl, combine spinach, strawberries, goat cheese, and almonds.
3. **Dress and Serve:**
     - Drizzle with olive oil and balsamic vinegar. Season with salt and pepper, toss gently, and serve immediately.

Roasted Sweet Potato Salad

Ingredients:

- 2 medium sweet potatoes, peeled and cubed
- 4 cups mixed greens
- 1/4 cup feta cheese, crumbled
- 1/4 cup pumpkin seeds
- 2 tablespoons olive oil
- 1 tablespoon honey
- Salt and pepper, to taste

Instructions:

1. **Roast the Sweet Potatoes:**
   - Preheat the oven to 400°F (200°C). Toss sweet potato cubes in olive oil, salt, and pepper. Roast for 25-30 minutes until tender.
2. **Prepare the Salad:**
   - In a large bowl, combine mixed greens, roasted sweet potatoes, feta, and pumpkin seeds.
3. **Make the Dressing:**
   - Whisk together olive oil and honey, then drizzle over the salad.
4. **Serve:**
   - Toss gently and serve immediately.

Asian Sesame Salad

Ingredients:

- 4 cups mixed greens (arugula, spinach, cabbage)
- 1 cup shredded carrots
- 1/2 cucumber, thinly sliced
- 1/4 cup sesame seeds
- 2 tablespoons soy sauce
- 1 tablespoon rice vinegar
- 1 tablespoon sesame oil
- 1 teaspoon honey
- Salt and pepper, to taste

Instructions:

1. **Prepare the Vegetables:**
    - Shred the carrots and slice the cucumber.
2. **Assemble the Salad:**
    - In a large bowl, toss mixed greens, carrots, cucumber, and sesame seeds.
3. **Make the Dressing:**
    - In a small bowl, whisk together soy sauce, rice vinegar, sesame oil, honey, salt, and pepper.
4. **Dress and Serve:**
    - Drizzle the dressing over the salad, toss, and serve immediately.

Tuna Nicoise Salad

Ingredients:

- 2 cans tuna in olive oil, drained
- 4 boiled eggs, quartered
- 1 cup green beans, blanched
- 1/2 cup cherry tomatoes, halved
- 1/4 cup Kalamata olives
- 4 cups mixed greens
- 2 tablespoons olive oil
- 1 tablespoon Dijon mustard
- 1 tablespoon red wine vinegar
- Salt and pepper, to taste

Instructions:

1. **Prepare the Ingredients:**
    - Boil the eggs and blanch the green beans.
2. **Assemble the Salad:**
    - In a large bowl, combine tuna, boiled eggs, green beans, tomatoes, olives, and mixed greens.
3. **Make the Dressing:**
    - Whisk together olive oil, Dijon mustard, red wine vinegar, salt, and pepper.
4. **Serve:**
    - Drizzle the dressing over the salad, toss gently, and serve immediately.

Mediterranean Orzo Salad

Ingredients:

- 2 cups cooked orzo pasta
- 1 cup cherry tomatoes, halved
- 1/2 cucumber, diced
- 1/4 cup Kalamata olives, sliced
- 1/4 cup red onion, thinly sliced
- 1/4 cup feta cheese, crumbled
- 2 tablespoons olive oil
- 1 tablespoon lemon juice
- 1 teaspoon oregano
- Salt and pepper, to taste

Instructions:

1. **Cook the Orzo:**
    - Cook orzo pasta according to package instructions and let cool.
2. **Combine the Ingredients:**
    - In a large bowl, combine orzo, tomatoes, cucumber, olives, red onion, and feta.
3. **Make the Dressing:**
    - Whisk together olive oil, lemon juice, oregano, salt, and pepper.
4. **Serve:**
    - Drizzle the dressing over the salad, toss gently, and serve immediately.

Thai Peanut Salad

Ingredients:

- 4 cups mixed greens (or napa cabbage)
- 1 cup shredded carrots
- 1/2 cucumber, julienned
- 1/4 red bell pepper, thinly sliced
- 1/4 cup cilantro, chopped
- 1/4 cup roasted peanuts, chopped
- 2 tablespoons sesame seeds

For the Peanut Dressing:

- 1/4 cup peanut butter
- 2 tablespoons soy sauce
- 1 tablespoon rice vinegar
- 1 tablespoon honey
- 1 teaspoon sesame oil
- 1 teaspoon lime juice
- 1/2 teaspoon grated ginger
- 1 clove garlic, minced

Instructions:

1. **Prepare the Salad:**
    - In a large bowl, combine the mixed greens, carrots, cucumber, bell pepper, cilantro, and peanuts.
2. **Make the Dressing:**
    - In a small bowl, whisk together peanut butter, soy sauce, rice vinegar, honey, sesame oil, lime juice, ginger, and garlic until smooth.
3. **Serve:**
    - Drizzle the dressing over the salad and sprinkle with sesame seeds. Toss gently and serve immediately.

Grilled Peach and Burrata Salad

Ingredients:

- 4 ripe peaches, halved and pitted
- 4 cups arugula or mixed greens
- 1 ball burrata cheese
- 1/4 cup toasted pine nuts
- 2 tablespoons balsamic glaze
- 2 tablespoons olive oil
- Salt and pepper, to taste

Instructions:

1. **Grill the Peaches:**
     - Preheat grill or grill pan to medium-high heat. Brush the peach halves with olive oil and grill for about 3-4 minutes on each side until charred and softened.
2. **Prepare the Salad:**
     - On a platter, arrange the arugula or mixed greens. Tear the burrata into pieces and place on the salad.
3. **Assemble the Salad:**
     - Add the grilled peaches, sprinkle with toasted pine nuts, drizzle with balsamic glaze, and season with salt and pepper.
4. **Serve:**
     - Toss gently and serve immediately.

Broccoli and Bacon Salad

Ingredients:

- 4 cups fresh broccoli florets, blanched
- 4 slices bacon, cooked and crumbled
- 1/2 cup red onion, finely chopped
- 1/2 cup shredded cheddar cheese
- 1/4 cup sunflower seeds

For the Dressing:

- 1/2 cup mayonnaise
- 2 tablespoons apple cider vinegar
- 1 tablespoon sugar
- Salt and pepper, to taste

Instructions:

1. **Prepare the Broccoli:**
   - Blanch the broccoli florets in boiling water for 2-3 minutes, then transfer them to an ice bath to cool. Drain well.
2. **Make the Dressing:**
   - In a small bowl, whisk together mayonnaise, apple cider vinegar, sugar, salt, and pepper.
3. **Assemble the Salad:**
   - In a large bowl, combine the broccoli, bacon, red onion, cheese, and sunflower seeds.
4. **Dress and Serve:**
   - Pour the dressing over the salad and toss to combine. Serve immediately.

Grilled Corn and Tomato Salad

Ingredients:

- 4 ears of corn, husked and grilled
- 2 cups cherry tomatoes, halved
- 1/4 cup red onion, thinly sliced
- 1/4 cup fresh cilantro, chopped
- 1 tablespoon lime juice
- 1 tablespoon olive oil
- Salt and pepper, to taste

Instructions:

1. **Grill the Corn:**
   - Preheat grill to medium-high. Grill the corn for 10-12 minutes, turning occasionally, until charred. Cut the kernels off the cob.
2. **Assemble the Salad:**
   - In a large bowl, combine grilled corn kernels, cherry tomatoes, red onion, and cilantro.
3. **Dress and Serve:**
   - Drizzle with lime juice and olive oil. Season with salt and pepper. Toss gently and serve immediately.

Panzanella (Italian Bread Salad)

Ingredients:

- 4 cups stale Italian bread, torn into chunks
- 2 cups cherry tomatoes, halved
- 1 cucumber, diced
- 1/2 red onion, thinly sliced
- 1/4 cup fresh basil, chopped
- 1/4 cup red wine vinegar
- 1/4 cup olive oil
- Salt and pepper, to taste

Instructions:

1. **Prepare the Bread:**
   - If the bread is not stale, toast it lightly in the oven to dry it out.
2. **Assemble the Salad:**
   - In a large bowl, combine the bread, tomatoes, cucumber, red onion, and basil.
3. **Dress and Serve:**
   - In a small bowl, whisk together red wine vinegar, olive oil, salt, and pepper. Drizzle over the salad and toss gently. Let sit for 10-15 minutes before serving to allow the bread to absorb the flavors.

Apple and Walnut Salad

Ingredients:

- 2 apples, cored and sliced
- 4 cups mixed greens (arugula, spinach, etc.)
- 1/4 cup walnuts, toasted
- 1/4 cup goat cheese, crumbled
- 2 tablespoons olive oil
- 1 tablespoon balsamic vinegar
- 1 teaspoon honey
- Salt and pepper, to taste

Instructions:

1. **Prepare the Salad:**
    - In a large bowl, combine the mixed greens, apple slices, toasted walnuts, and goat cheese.
2. **Make the Dressing:**
    - In a small bowl, whisk together olive oil, balsamic vinegar, honey, salt, and pepper.
3. **Dress and Serve:**
    - Drizzle the dressing over the salad, toss gently, and serve immediately.

Farro and Roasted Carrot Salad

Ingredients:

- 1 cup farro, cooked
- 4 large carrots, peeled and sliced
- 2 tablespoons olive oil
- 1/4 cup feta cheese, crumbled
- 1/4 cup fresh parsley, chopped
- 1 tablespoon lemon juice
- Salt and pepper, to taste

Instructions:

1. **Roast the Carrots:**
    - Preheat oven to 400°F (200°C). Toss the sliced carrots with olive oil, salt, and pepper. Roast for 20-25 minutes until tender.
2. **Prepare the Salad:**
    - In a large bowl, combine the cooked farro, roasted carrots, feta cheese, and parsley.
3. **Dress and Serve:**
    - Drizzle with lemon juice, toss gently, and serve immediately.

Beetroot and Walnut Salad

Ingredients:

- 4 medium beets, roasted and peeled
- 4 cups mixed greens (spinach, arugula, etc.)
- 1/4 cup walnuts, toasted
- 1/4 cup goat cheese, crumbled
- 2 tablespoons olive oil
- 1 tablespoon balsamic vinegar
- Salt and pepper, to taste

Instructions:

1. **Roast the Beets:**
    - Preheat oven to 400°F (200°C). Wrap beets in foil and roast for 45-60 minutes until tender. Peel and slice.
2. **Assemble the Salad:**
    - In a large bowl, combine the mixed greens, roasted beets, walnuts, and goat cheese.
3. **Dress and Serve:**
    - Drizzle with olive oil and balsamic vinegar. Season with salt and pepper. Toss gently and serve immediately.

Brussels Sprout and Pomegranate Salad

Ingredients:

- 4 cups Brussels sprouts, shredded
- 1/2 cup pomegranate seeds
- 1/4 cup feta cheese, crumbled
- 2 tablespoons olive oil
- 1 tablespoon apple cider vinegar
- 1 teaspoon Dijon mustard
- Salt and pepper, to taste

Instructions:

1. **Prepare the Brussels Sprouts:**
   - Shred the Brussels sprouts using a mandoline or sharp knife.
2. **Make the Dressing:**
   - In a small bowl, whisk together olive oil, apple cider vinegar, Dijon mustard, salt, and pepper.
3. **Assemble the Salad:**
   - In a large bowl, combine shredded Brussels sprouts, pomegranate seeds, and feta.
4. **Dress and Serve:**
   - Drizzle with dressing and toss gently. Serve immediately.

Cabbage and Radish Slaw

Ingredients:

- 4 cups shredded cabbage
- 1 cup radishes, thinly sliced
- 1/4 cup green onions, chopped
- 1/4 cup fresh parsley, chopped
- 2 tablespoons apple cider vinegar
- 1 tablespoon olive oil
- 1 teaspoon Dijon mustard
- 1 teaspoon honey
- Salt and pepper, to taste

Instructions:

1. **Prepare the Slaw:**
    - In a large bowl, combine the shredded cabbage, radishes, green onions, and parsley.
2. **Make the Dressing:**
    - In a small bowl, whisk together the apple cider vinegar, olive oil, Dijon mustard, honey, salt, and pepper.
3. **Toss and Serve:**
    - Pour the dressing over the cabbage mixture and toss gently to combine. Serve immediately or chill for 20 minutes before serving.

Shrimp and Avocado Salad

Ingredients:

- 1 lb cooked shrimp, peeled and deveined
- 2 avocados, diced
- 1 cup cherry tomatoes, halved
- 1/4 cup red onion, thinly sliced
- 1 tablespoon fresh cilantro, chopped
- 1 tablespoon lime juice
- 2 tablespoons olive oil
- Salt and pepper, to taste

Instructions:

1. **Prepare the Salad:**
    - In a large bowl, combine shrimp, avocados, cherry tomatoes, red onion, and cilantro.
2. **Dress and Serve:**
    - Drizzle with lime juice and olive oil, and season with salt and pepper. Toss gently and serve immediately.

Lemon and Herb Potato Salad

Ingredients:

- 1 1/2 lbs baby potatoes, boiled and halved
- 1/4 cup fresh parsley, chopped
- 2 tablespoons fresh dill, chopped
- 1 tablespoon lemon juice
- 1 teaspoon lemon zest
- 2 tablespoons olive oil
- Salt and pepper, to taste

Instructions:

1. **Prepare the Potatoes:**
   - Boil the potatoes until tender, about 10-12 minutes. Drain and let cool slightly.
2. **Make the Dressing:**
   - In a small bowl, whisk together lemon juice, lemon zest, olive oil, salt, and pepper.
3. **Assemble the Salad:**
   - Toss the warm potatoes with the dressing, parsley, and dill. Season with additional salt and pepper, if desired. Serve warm or chilled.

Grilled Zucchini and Halloumi Salad

Ingredients:

- 2 zucchinis, sliced into 1/2-inch rounds
- 1 block Halloumi cheese, sliced
- 2 tablespoons olive oil
- 1 tablespoon lemon juice
- 1 teaspoon dried oregano
- Salt and pepper, to taste
- Fresh basil, chopped (for garnish)

Instructions:

1. **Grill the Vegetables:**
    - Preheat the grill to medium-high heat. Brush the zucchini and Halloumi slices with olive oil. Grill the zucchini for 3-4 minutes per side and the Halloumi for 2-3 minutes per side, until grill marks appear.
2. **Assemble the Salad:**
    - In a serving platter, arrange the grilled zucchini and Halloumi. Drizzle with lemon juice, sprinkle with oregano, and season with salt and pepper.
3. **Serve:**
    - Garnish with fresh basil and serve immediately.

Cucumber, Dill, and Yogurt Salad

Ingredients:

- 2 cucumbers, thinly sliced
- 1/2 cup Greek yogurt
- 2 tablespoons fresh dill, chopped
- 1 tablespoon lemon juice
- 1 tablespoon olive oil
- Salt and pepper, to taste

Instructions:

1. **Prepare the Salad:**
    - In a large bowl, combine the sliced cucumbers and chopped dill.
2. **Make the Dressing:**
    - In a small bowl, whisk together Greek yogurt, lemon juice, olive oil, salt, and pepper.
3. **Serve:**
    - Pour the dressing over the cucumbers, toss gently, and serve immediately.

Carrot and Chickpea Salad

Ingredients:

- 3 large carrots, peeled and grated
- 1 can (15 oz) chickpeas, drained and rinsed
- 1/4 cup fresh parsley, chopped
- 1/4 cup olive oil
- 2 tablespoons lemon juice
- 1 teaspoon ground cumin
- Salt and pepper, to taste

Instructions:

1. **Prepare the Salad:**
    - In a large bowl, combine the grated carrots, chickpeas, and parsley.
2. **Make the Dressing:**
    - In a small bowl, whisk together olive oil, lemon juice, cumin, salt, and pepper.
3. **Toss and Serve:**
    - Drizzle the dressing over the salad, toss to combine, and serve immediately.

Poppy Seed and Apple Salad

Ingredients:

- 2 apples, cored and sliced
- 4 cups mixed greens (arugula, spinach, etc.)
- 1/4 cup toasted pecans
- 2 tablespoons poppy seeds
- 1/4 cup feta cheese, crumbled

For the Dressing:

- 2 tablespoons apple cider vinegar
- 1 tablespoon Dijon mustard
- 1 tablespoon honey
- 3 tablespoons olive oil
- Salt and pepper, to taste

Instructions:

1. **Prepare the Salad:**
    - In a large bowl, combine the mixed greens, apple slices, toasted pecans, and feta.
2. **Make the Dressing:**
    - In a small bowl, whisk together apple cider vinegar, Dijon mustard, honey, olive oil, salt, and pepper.
3. **Dress and Serve:**
    - Drizzle the dressing over the salad, sprinkle with poppy seeds, and toss gently to serve.

Roasted Brussels Sprout Salad

Ingredients:

- 4 cups Brussels sprouts, trimmed and halved
- 2 tablespoons olive oil
- Salt and pepper, to taste
- 1/4 cup dried cranberries
- 1/4 cup toasted walnuts
- 2 tablespoons balsamic vinegar

Instructions:

1. **Roast the Brussels Sprouts:**
    - Preheat the oven to 400°F (200°C). Toss the halved Brussels sprouts with olive oil, salt, and pepper. Roast for 20-25 minutes until tender and crispy on the edges.
2. **Assemble the Salad:**
    - In a large bowl, combine the roasted Brussels sprouts, cranberries, and toasted walnuts.
3. **Dress and Serve:**
    - Drizzle with balsamic vinegar, toss gently, and serve warm or at room temperature.

Spinach and Bacon Salad

Ingredients:

- 4 cups fresh spinach
- 4 slices bacon, cooked and crumbled
- 1/4 cup red onion, thinly sliced
- 1/4 cup boiled eggs, chopped
- 1/4 cup blue cheese, crumbled
- 1 tablespoon olive oil
- 1 tablespoon red wine vinegar
- Salt and pepper, to taste

Instructions:

1. **Prepare the Salad:**
    - In a large bowl, combine the spinach, bacon, red onion, boiled eggs, and blue cheese.
2. **Make the Dressing:**
    - In a small bowl, whisk together olive oil, red wine vinegar, salt, and pepper.
3. **Dress and Serve:**
    - Drizzle the dressing over the salad, toss gently, and serve immediately.

Warm Lentil Salad with Goat Cheese

Ingredients:

- 1 cup green or brown lentils, rinsed
- 1 small red onion, finely chopped
- 2 tablespoons olive oil
- 1/4 cup fresh parsley, chopped
- 1/4 cup goat cheese, crumbled
- 2 tablespoons red wine vinegar
- 1 tablespoon Dijon mustard
- Salt and pepper, to taste

Instructions:

1. **Cook the Lentils:**
    - In a medium saucepan, cook the lentils in salted water according to package directions until tender, about 20-25 minutes. Drain and set aside.
2. **Prepare the Dressing:**
    - In a small bowl, whisk together olive oil, red wine vinegar, Dijon mustard, salt, and pepper.
3. **Assemble the Salad:**
    - In a large bowl, combine the warm lentils, red onion, and parsley. Drizzle with the dressing and toss gently.
4. **Serve:**
    - Top with crumbled goat cheese and serve warm.

Grilled Chicken and Mango Salad

Ingredients:

- 2 chicken breasts, grilled and sliced
- 1 mango, peeled and diced
- 4 cups mixed greens (arugula, spinach, etc.)
- 1/4 cup red onion, thinly sliced
- 1/4 cup fresh cilantro, chopped
- 1 tablespoon olive oil
- 1 tablespoon lime juice
- Salt and pepper, to taste

Instructions:

1. **Grill the Chicken:**
    - Season the chicken breasts with salt and pepper and grill until fully cooked, about 6-7 minutes per side. Slice the chicken into strips.
2. **Prepare the Salad:**
    - In a large bowl, combine the mixed greens, diced mango, red onion, and cilantro.
3. **Dress and Serve:**
    - Drizzle with olive oil and lime juice, toss to combine, and top with grilled chicken. Serve immediately.

Roasted Cauliflower and Tahini Salad

Ingredients:

- 1 head of cauliflower, cut into florets
- 2 tablespoons olive oil
- Salt and pepper, to taste
- 1/4 cup tahini
- 1 tablespoon lemon juice
- 1 teaspoon garlic, minced
- 2 tablespoons water (to thin out the dressing)
- 2 tablespoons fresh parsley, chopped

Instructions:

1. **Roast the Cauliflower:**
   - Preheat the oven to 400°F (200°C). Toss the cauliflower florets with olive oil, salt, and pepper. Roast for 20-25 minutes until golden brown and tender.
2. **Prepare the Dressing:**
   - In a small bowl, whisk together tahini, lemon juice, garlic, water, salt, and pepper until smooth.
3. **Assemble the Salad:**
   - In a serving bowl, combine the roasted cauliflower and fresh parsley. Drizzle with the tahini dressing and toss gently.
4. **Serve:**
   - Serve warm or at room temperature.

Fennel and Orange Salad

Ingredients:

- 2 fennel bulbs, thinly sliced
- 2 oranges, peeled and segmented
- 1 tablespoon olive oil
- 1 tablespoon white wine vinegar
- Salt and pepper, to taste
- 1/4 cup fresh mint leaves, chopped

Instructions:

1. **Prepare the Salad:**
    - In a large bowl, combine the fennel slices and orange segments.
2. **Dress and Serve:**
    - Drizzle with olive oil and white wine vinegar, then season with salt and pepper. Toss gently to combine.
3. **Garnish:**
    - Sprinkle with fresh mint leaves and serve immediately.

Spinach and Quinoa Salad

Ingredients:

- 1 cup quinoa, cooked
- 4 cups fresh spinach
- 1/4 cup red onion, thinly sliced
- 1/4 cup feta cheese, crumbled
- 1/4 cup walnuts, chopped
- 1 tablespoon olive oil
- 1 tablespoon balsamic vinegar
- Salt and pepper, to taste

Instructions:

1. **Cook the Quinoa:**
    - Cook the quinoa according to package directions and let it cool.
2. **Assemble the Salad:**
    - In a large bowl, combine the cooked quinoa, fresh spinach, red onion, feta cheese, and walnuts.
3. **Dress and Serve:**
    - Drizzle with olive oil and balsamic vinegar, toss gently, and season with salt and pepper. Serve immediately.

Roasted Pumpkin and Kale Salad

Ingredients:

- 1 small pumpkin, peeled and cubed
- 2 tablespoons olive oil
- Salt and pepper, to taste
- 4 cups kale, chopped
- 1/4 cup goat cheese, crumbled
- 1/4 cup pumpkin seeds, toasted
- 1 tablespoon apple cider vinegar

Instructions:

1. **Roast the Pumpkin:**
    - Preheat the oven to 400°F (200°C). Toss the cubed pumpkin with olive oil, salt, and pepper. Roast for 20-25 minutes until tender and lightly browned.
2. **Prepare the Salad:**
    - In a large bowl, massage the chopped kale with apple cider vinegar for 1-2 minutes to soften.
3. **Assemble the Salad:**
    - Add the roasted pumpkin, goat cheese, and pumpkin seeds to the kale. Toss gently and serve immediately.

Strawberry and Almond Salad

Ingredients:

- 2 cups fresh strawberries, hulled and sliced
- 4 cups mixed greens (arugula, spinach, etc.)
- 1/4 cup sliced almonds, toasted
- 1 tablespoon balsamic vinegar
- 1 tablespoon honey
- 1 tablespoon olive oil
- Salt and pepper, to taste

Instructions:

1. **Prepare the Salad:**
   - In a large bowl, combine the strawberries and mixed greens.
2. **Make the Dressing:**
   - In a small bowl, whisk together balsamic vinegar, honey, olive oil, salt, and pepper.
3. **Dress and Serve:**
   - Drizzle the dressing over the salad, toss gently, and top with toasted almonds. Serve immediately.

Roasted Vegetable and Couscous Salad

Ingredients:

- 1 cup couscous
- 2 cups mixed vegetables (carrots, bell peppers, zucchini, eggplant), chopped
- 2 tablespoons olive oil
- Salt and pepper, to taste
- 1/4 cup fresh parsley, chopped
- 1/4 cup feta cheese, crumbled (optional)
- 2 tablespoons lemon juice
- 1 tablespoon balsamic vinegar

Instructions:

1. **Roast the Vegetables:**
    - Preheat the oven to 400°F (200°C). Toss the chopped vegetables with olive oil, salt, and pepper. Roast for 20-25 minutes until tender and lightly browned.
2. **Prepare the Couscous:**
    - In a medium saucepan, bring 1 1/4 cups of water to a boil. Add the couscous, cover, and remove from heat. Let it steam for 5 minutes, then fluff with a fork.
3. **Assemble the Salad:**
    - In a large bowl, combine the couscous, roasted vegetables, parsley, and feta (if using).
4. **Dress and Serve:**
    - Drizzle with lemon juice and balsamic vinegar. Toss gently and serve warm or at room temperature.

Shrimp and Grapefruit Salad

Ingredients:

- 1 pound cooked shrimp, peeled and deveined
- 2 grapefruits, peeled and segmented
- 4 cups mixed greens (arugula, spinach, etc.)
- 1/4 cup red onion, thinly sliced
- 1 tablespoon olive oil
- 1 tablespoon honey
- 1 tablespoon white wine vinegar
- Salt and pepper, to taste

Instructions:

1. **Prepare the Salad:**
   - In a large bowl, combine the shrimp, grapefruit segments, mixed greens, and red onion.
2. **Make the Dressing:**
   - In a small bowl, whisk together olive oil, honey, white wine vinegar, salt, and pepper.
3. **Dress and Serve:**
   - Drizzle the dressing over the salad, toss gently, and serve immediately.

Lentil and Avocado Salad

Ingredients:

- 1 cup cooked lentils
- 2 ripe avocados, diced
- 1/4 cup red onion, finely chopped
- 1/4 cup fresh cilantro, chopped
- 1 tablespoon olive oil
- 1 tablespoon lime juice
- Salt and pepper, to taste

Instructions:

1. **Prepare the Salad:**
   - In a large bowl, combine the cooked lentils, avocado, red onion, and cilantro.
2. **Dress and Serve:**
   - Drizzle with olive oil and lime juice, toss gently, and season with salt and pepper. Serve immediately.

Cucumber and Tomato Salad

Ingredients:

- 2 cups cucumber, sliced
- 2 cups cherry tomatoes, halved
- 1/4 cup red onion, thinly sliced
- 2 tablespoons olive oil
- 1 tablespoon red wine vinegar
- 1 tablespoon fresh dill, chopped
- Salt and pepper, to taste

Instructions:

1. **Prepare the Salad:**
    - In a large bowl, combine the cucumber, cherry tomatoes, and red onion.
2. **Dress and Serve:**
    - Drizzle with olive oil and red wine vinegar, toss gently, and season with fresh dill, salt, and pepper. Serve immediately.

Apple, Beet, and Walnut Salad

Ingredients:

- 2 apples, sliced
- 2 cups roasted beets, peeled and chopped
- 1/4 cup walnuts, toasted
- 4 cups arugula or mixed greens
- 2 tablespoons olive oil
- 1 tablespoon apple cider vinegar
- 1 teaspoon honey
- Salt and pepper, to taste

Instructions:

1. **Prepare the Salad:**
    - In a large bowl, combine the sliced apples, roasted beets, walnuts, and mixed greens.
2. **Make the Dressing:**
    - In a small bowl, whisk together olive oil, apple cider vinegar, honey, salt, and pepper.
3. **Dress and Serve:**
    - Drizzle the dressing over the salad, toss gently, and serve immediately.

Pear and Blue Cheese Salad

Ingredients:

- 2 pears, sliced
- 1/4 cup crumbled blue cheese
- 1/4 cup candied pecans or walnuts
- 4 cups mixed greens
- 2 tablespoons olive oil
- 1 tablespoon balsamic vinegar
- Salt and pepper, to taste

Instructions:

1. **Prepare the Salad:**
    - In a large bowl, combine the sliced pears, blue cheese, candied nuts, and mixed greens.
2. **Dress and Serve:**
    - Drizzle with olive oil and balsamic vinegar, toss gently, and season with salt and pepper. Serve immediately.

Roasted Tomato and Pesto Salad

Ingredients:

- 2 cups cherry tomatoes, halved
- 1/4 cup pesto sauce (store-bought or homemade)
- 2 tablespoons olive oil
- Salt and pepper, to taste
- 1/4 cup fresh basil leaves, chopped

Instructions:

1. **Roast the Tomatoes:**
    - Preheat the oven to 375°F (190°C). Toss the halved cherry tomatoes with olive oil, salt, and pepper. Roast for 15-20 minutes until soft and caramelized.
2. **Prepare the Salad:**
    - In a large bowl, combine the roasted tomatoes with pesto sauce.
3. **Garnish and Serve:**
    - Top with fresh basil and serve warm or at room temperature.

www.ingramcontent.com/pod-product-compliance
Lightning Source LLC
LaVergne TN
LVHW081337060526
838201LV00055B/2707